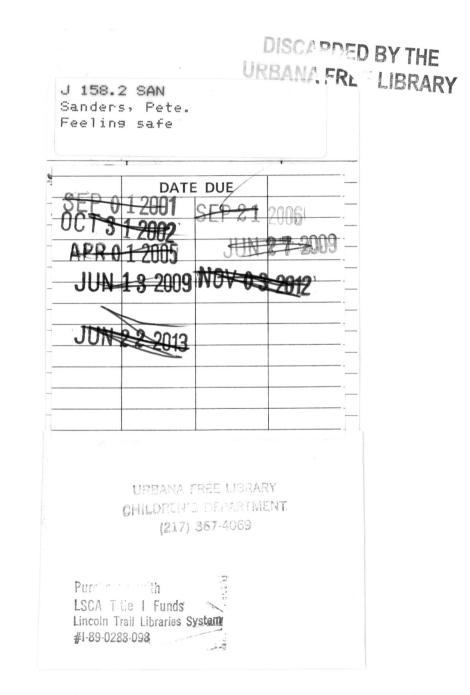

FEELING SAFE

© Aladdin Books Ltd 1988

Designed and produced by
Aladdin Books Ltd, 70 Old Compton Street, London W1V 5PA

Editor: Catherine Bradley
Design: Rob Hillier
Research: Cecilia Weston-Baker
Consultant: Angela Grunsell

Pete Sanders is the head teacher of a North London
primary school and is working with groups of teachers
on personal, social and health education.

Angela Grunsell is an advisory teacher specializing in
development education and resources for the primary
school age range.

Published in the United States in 1988 by
Gloucester Press, 387 Park Avenue South, New York, NY 10016

ISBN 0 531 17081 0

Library of Congress Catalog
Card Number: 87 82885

Printed in Belgium

"LET'S TALK ABOUT"

FEELING SAFE

PETE SANDERS

Gloucester Press
New York · London · Toronto · Sydney

"How can I make sure that I feel safe and don't get hurt?"

Feeling safe is about making sure you feel and keep well. It's easy to get into a situation where you may be upset, so you need to know how to look after yourself.

It's your right to be safe and happy. Often the reason you feel happy is that you're doing something you want to do.

> Most people enjoy sharing something with a friend – it can make them feel happy.

When you're feeling hurt, it's nice to have someone to talk to. You may sometimes feel like crying.

"When does it hurt?"

It hurts when you or your body feel pain. Sometimes it's an illness. Sometimes it's because you're upset. You can get hurt by mistake, by something you can't control, like in an accident. But sometimes you get hurt because other people are unkind. Maybe your best friend seems friendly with someone else and is ignoring you.

When you're feeling upset, it often helps to **talk** to someone about it. Sometimes that's the **only** way anyone is going to know about your pain.

7

"How are people unkind?"

People can be unkind without meaning to be. You may have hurt someone yourself. You may not have wanted to be cruel but it happened. But sometimes you get angry and you want to hurt someone. Maybe it's because you think they're hurting you.

Some people seem to enjoy making fun of anybody who's different. They can be cruel about all kinds of things, like the way people dress or talk or because their skin is a different color.

8

Other children can hurt you without realizing it.

9

"Why are people unkind?"

There are lots of reasons people are unkind. Maybe it's because someone's been mean to them and so they take it out on you.

Another time it could be that some children want to be part of a group or gang. To be accepted by the gang, they may do things which they wouldn't do normally. They join in because everyone else is doing it. If they said how they felt, they might find that others in the gang agree with them.

It can be great fun being in a gang.
But the gang may make you do things
you don't want to do.

You can feel very lonely when someone is bullying you but it's important to talk about it. If you don't, then the bully will get away with it and no one will help you.

Bullies often act big because they think it's important to look tough. They think that's the only way to get friends. They like to be able to control people and feel powerful.

There are lots of ways of coping with bullies. Some children get together with their friends, so they can say no. Others make sure they stay out of the bully's way.

Like you, bullies are only trying to get friends. They need help. But bullies scare you so you don't tell anyone. If you don't talk about it, then neither you nor the bully will ever get help.

"What if someone's trying to get at me?"

Some boys enjoy making fun of girls. They think they can pester them and make rude remarks simply because they are girls. Some girls put up with this because they think they should. Instead they should trust how they feel and do something about it.

Boys sometimes feel that they have to act strong and put up with pain. They want to look brave, even when they don't feel it. You don't have to be so hard on yourself – just go with your feelings and express them.

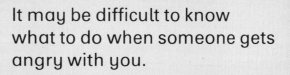

It may be difficult to know what to do when someone gets angry with you.

"How do I know if people are as nice as they appear to be?"

Sometimes people try to talk to children they don't know. They may just want to be friendly. However you've got to think carefully before you talk to a stranger.

Some people who are older try to trick children into going with them. They might offer candy or a ride in a car as a bribe. Just because someone is older, it doesn't mean you have to do what they say. If a stranger tries to talk to you, it's OK to ignore the stranger.

Always think carefully before accepting a lift with someone else, whether you know them or not. Play it safe.

"But what about people I know well? Can they hurt me?"

It can happen that people who care for you are unkind to you for your own good. But some people are not doing it for your well-being. It's hard to tell the difference. You can learn to do this and trust your own feelings. The best way to find out how to do this is by sharing your ideas with friends and people you trust.

Sometimes you may think that people who care for you are unkind. They might hit you. They may say they are doing it for your own good. By scolding you they may be saying that they care.

"Are some people unkind to me on purpose?"

A few people may actually use you to get something they want. These people involve you in things that feel very uncomfortable. They say it's just a game.

But the games they play involve tickling, kissing and touching in ways which might upset you. They try to frighten you into not saying anything about what is happening. They tell you that whatever is going on is a secret. But it's their secret, not yours.

Some secrets are fun, and they are OK between friends and family. But some secrets are bad — they are the ones that make you feel mixed up. That's when you need to talk.

"What can I do to stop someone from hurting me?"

If someone is doing something to you which hurts, like hitting you or touching you in ways you don't like, then you have every right to say "stop it." You can say no to grown-ups – even your parents – if they're doing something wrong.

If you keep it a secret, whoever is hurting you can get away with it. If you're feeling mixed up, frightened or worried, you need to talk, maybe to a teacher. It is your right to feel safe.

Feeling on your own can be very frightening. If someone's hurting you, it makes you feel very cut off. Keeping it a secret will not make it go away. If someone scares you into keeping a bad secret, talk about it to an adult.

GOING ROUND IN CIRCLES

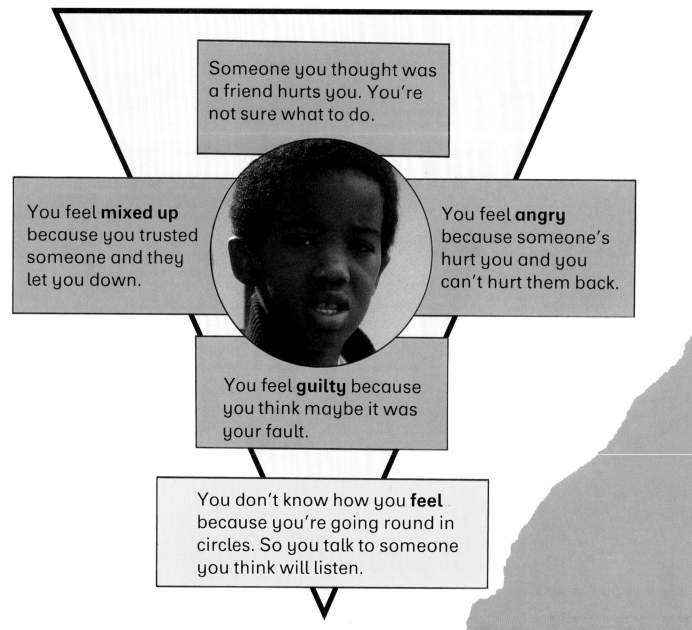

Someone you thought was a friend hurts you. You're not sure what to do.

You feel **mixed up** because you trusted someone and they let you down.

You feel **angry** because someone's hurt you and you can't hurt them back.

You feel **guilty** because you think maybe it was your fault.

You don't know how you **feel** because you're going round in circles. So you talk to someone you think will listen.

"How do I find a way to talk about things that upset me?"

Sometimes it's hard to talk about things that upset you, especially if you think no one is going to believe you. But most adults will understand and want to help. Remember it's the one who's doing the hurting who is wrong, not the one who is being hurt.

You're often told that grown-ups know better. This may be true for lots of things, but not always. No one has the right to hurt you — adult or child.

25

If it's difficult to talk to your parents you could try an older brother or sister, a neighbor, a family friend, or a teacher.

"What if no one will listen to me?"

Sometimes it seems like everyone is too busy to stop and listen to you. It may be that the first person you talk to doesn't know what to say when you tell them what's wrong. If that happens, then it's important to find someone else to talk to.

It's important to keep on talking. It may be painful and difficult. But in the end, it's less painful than being hurt all the time. By talking you may prevent someone else from being hurt too.

"So I should be able to keep on feeling safe if I trust my feelings?"

No one should hurt you on purpose or force you to do something that hurts. You've got the right to be happy and do what you want to do, as long as it doesn't hurt anyone.

You need to know how to look after yourself. Often it's a case of being aware of the world around you and knowing what to do in certain situations. Feeling safe is about knowing your feelings and sharing them with others. It's your right to be safe and stay happy.

It feels safe when you know someone's there you can rely on. But it also feels safe when you know how to look after yourself.

"What can I do?"

There are lots of ways of looking after yourself and making sure you feel safe. For example, always tell adults you trust where you are going. It's useful to know how to make telephone calls and how to answer them. Some families use special code words, which they use with each other so they know who they can trust.

You've got rights which others have to respect. You've got the right to be happy. As you get older, you learn to make choices. To do this, you need to share your beliefs and views with those you can trust. In this way, you learn from each other.

Your Rights

You have the right to be loved, to have education, nourishing food, enough sleep, warmth, peace and privacy, play with other children, space to play in and space to explore.

If you're in trouble, ask for help. Don't keep your troubles to yourself. Most people will try to help you, if you ask them to. Keep trying until someone listens. If you can't find anyone to talk to then, you can ring these numbers for help:

International Institute of Children's Nature and Rights
1615 Myrtle St NW
Washington DC   20012
(202) 726 3341

Childhelp USA International
6463 Independence Avenue
Woodland Hills, CA 91370
(818) 347 7280

Index

Photographic Credits:
Cover and pages 4-5: Camilla
Jessel; pages 6, 11, 12-13, 21, 23,
26 and 29: Sally and Richard
Greenhill; pages 8-9 and 15:
Network Photographers; page 15:
Rex Features; page 18: Anthea
Sieveking/Vision International.